Bloom

Poems that Speak to One's Soul

by

Terri L. McCrea, M.Ed., LPC

Bloom: Poems that Speak to One's Soul

Cassaundra Mulligan, Editor

Cover and interior arrangements - by Kathrine Rend
Rend Graphics www.rendgraphics.com

Printed in the United States of America.

ISBN: 978-1-7376194-3-7

Poetic Expressions by Terri
Terri L. McCrea, M.Ed., LPC, LPC/S
1643 B Savannah Highway, #113
Charleston, SC 29407
Mobile (843) 437-7572
Fax (843) 763-7202
poeticexpressions@att.net

Introduction

This second poetry collection evolved in 2019 during one of the darkest periods of this century. In the blink of an eye, a mutation called Coronavirus, created mayhem, panic and resulted in worldwide mass casualties.

Bloom's poems materialized while grappling with the how's and why's of these surreal events and in processing how overnight, a deadly virus could hold the world captive.

I pray the poems, in *Bloom*, can transform the readers darkness into light, sadness into joy, confusion into clarity, anger into forgiveness and gloom into hope.

I challenge the reader, to get not only, their house, their family, their life calling, their time, their marriage, their heart, but most importantly, their soul in order.

I define living as a phenomenon where souls vacillate through their visions, dreams and organic intentions with clarity and butterfly love. I hope the poems in *Bloom* motivate the reader to stop existing and start living with mindfulness, peace and purpose.

Acknowledgements

I would like to thank each person, place, event and thing that inspired, supported and breathed life in the making of this second, but certainly, not my last collection of poetry.

Bloom captures the depths and landscape of life, especially during these precarious times.

I would like to thank my young creatives and those grieving souls for sharing their survival stories during this season of adaptation.

I thank you from the bottom of my heart.

Contents

Bloom

Poems that Speak to One's Soul

Your Name is Freedom

Don't fret, because you are his sheep.

Your being is not to be feared,
It is to be respected.

You are not less than, you are a gift.

Your living won't be in vain,
It will be purposeful.

Your name is not nigga,
It is neighbor, brotha, King.

Your spirit can't be broken, it's resilient.

Your name is not Jezebel,
It is sista, goddess, Queen.

Your temple is not to be the object
of another's projection, it is holy.

Your soul is not of hate or rage, it is of love.

You are not a slave, they enslaved.

Embrace your name.
It is Epiphany
It is Strength
It is Trinity
It is Freedom.

Awake With the Purpose To

Awake with the purpose to help and to heal.
Awake with the purpose
to be resilient against the unpredictable,
the indoctrinated and the surreal.

Awake with the purpose
to encourage and to elevate.
Awake with purpose
to uplift and to celebrate.

Awake with the purpose
to transform and to teach.
Awake with the purpose
to pray for and to reach.

Awake with the purpose
to unify and to unite.
Awake with the purpose
to empower and to inspire.

Awake with the purpose
to mend hearts and to touch.
Awake with the purpose
to uplift and to love.

Awake with the purpose
to awaken and to grow.
Awake with the purpose
to honor all heavenly and
connect with all earthly souls.

If I Had a Magic Wand, I Would Heal the World

If I had a magic wand, I would heal the world's
Ignorance
&
Dissonance.

If I had a magic wand, I would heal the world's
Misguided Youth
&
Illusions from Mistruths.

If I had a magic wand, I would heal the world's
Discontent
&
Wailing Lament.

If I had a magic wand, I would heal the world's
Broken
&
Commotion.

If I had a magic wand, I would heal the world's
Toxic Legacies
&
Contrary Hypocrisies.

If I had a magic wand, I would heal the world's
Subliminal Fallacy
&
Slave Mentalities.

If I had a magic wand, I would heal the world's
Chaotic ness
&
Fleeing Madness.

If I had a magic wand, I would heal the world's
Narcissm
&
Delusional Realism.

If I had a magic wand, I would heal the world's
Passivity
&
Cruel Inhumanity.

If I had a magic wand, I would heal the world's
Ingrained Denial
&
Adversity, Suffering and Burdening Trials.

If I had a magic wand, I would heal the world's
Enraged
&
Disengaged.

If I had a magic wand, I would heal the world's
Envy
&
Jealousy.

If I had a magic wand, I would heal
the world.

Living

Living is
vascillating through
one's visions, dreams
&
organic intentions with
butterfly love.

Life Aint Fair

Cancer ain't fair.
Death ain't fair.
Discrimination ain't fair.
Dead beat parents ain't fair.
Natural Disasters ain't fair.
Deportation ain't fair.
Hate ain't fair.
Poverty ain't fair.
Racial Profiling ain't fair.
Politicking ain't fair.
Bullying ain't fair.
Covid-19 ain't fair.
Man's Inhumanity to Man ain't fair.

Life ain't fair,
but turning one's adversity into
a timeless passion can breathe
hope, healing and light into the injustice.

It's Time...

It's Time for Living not just Existing,
for Surrendering not Resisting.

It's Time for Humility not Pridefulness,
for Compassion not Idleness.

It's Time for Togetherness
not Dissonance,
for Harmony not Divisiveness.

It's Time for Persisting
not Procrastinating,
for Healing not Invalidating.

It's Time for Unity not Mutiny,
for Transparency not Opacity.

It's Time for Forgiveness not Blame,
for Acceptance not Shame.

It's Time for Self-Reflection
not Deflection,
for Growth not Regression.

It's Time for Love not Hate,
for Prayer, Hope and Faith.

It's Time for Peace not War,
to Bloom, Fly and Soar.

Isn't it Time?

Just Listen

If you desire to capture a woman's heart, just listen.

Listen to her thoughts.
Get lost in her visions.
Listen to her beautiful dreams
while supporting her
selfless missions.

Listen carefully to her wants,
her desires
and her needs.
Empathize with her pain.
Listen to her soul's intentions
as you walk beside her in the
down pour of rain.

Listen to her hurts.
Adore the sparkle in her eyes.
Listen to the inflection in her voice.
Relish in her blossoming passions
as she beamingly smiles.

Be awe struck by her creativity
while supporting her steps.
Be awe struck by her glow
as she articulates her depth.

Empower her sense of self.
Embrace her truths.
Be captivated by her joys while allowing her to see the vulnerable,
the emotionally available and the authentic you.

Jalen

Tell the world not how he died but how
within his seeds he will live.
Tell his kids how to his last penny
he would selflessly give.
Tell the world that the mindless
senselessness has to end.
Tell his kids it's okay to cry
while their broken hearts mend.
Tell the world you won't rest
until there is resounding justice.
Tell his kids that there will
always be a story of an us.
Tell the world of his old soul
that was full of wisdom and depth.
Tell his kids to walk in his
honorable, intentional and brave footsteps.
Tell the world about his
pure, golden and caring heart.
Tell his kids that they were the inspiration behind his moving works of art.
Tell the world how he fills every fiber of your being with pride and joy.
Tell his kids that their free-spirited souls
will always possess a nostalgic aura.
Tell the world her Guardian Angel
now has his wings.
Tell his kids that he will be the reason
why grandma hums and sings.
Tell the world how forgiveness will rise
from the merciless deed.
Tell his kids that dad will speak to them
in their sweet sweet dreams.

Tell the world how he was a bright
luminous star.
Tell his kids that their dad will never be afar.
Tell the world that he walked
passionately and in peace.
Tell his kids to honor him
every second, of every minute,
of every day, of every week.
Tell the world of how your baby boy transformed
from a prince into a valiant king.
Tell his kids to never forget
the love that emitted from his eyes
when they walked in a room,
during their moments of mourn,
during their moments of glee and
during their moments of reminisce.

He Empowers

He empowers me to fly.
He empowers me to soar.
He empowers the drive
behind my dreams.
He empowers my steps
while journeying through
life's doors.

He empowers my passions.
He empowers my hopeful heart.
He empowers my thriving soul.
He empowers the vision behind
my moving works of art.

He empowers my resilience.
He empowers my organic empathy.
He empowers my mindfulness.
He empowers my authenticity.

He empowers the strength
of my intuition.
He empowers my fearless drive.
He empowers my inevitable destiny.
He empowers my valuable, my gifted,
my deserving and my worthy life.

My Life

When lost in translation
about your life,
know that what truly matters
is not your beginning,
but the amazing chapters in between
and it's beautiful ending.

When

When Feeling Hurt or Scarred,
Whisper, I Am Healed.

When Feeling Disappointed,
Whisper, I Am Satisfied and I Am Grateful.

When Feeling Incomplete or Empty,
Whisper, I Am Complete and I Am Whole.

When Feeling Frustrated,
Whisper, I Am a Glow-Getter and I Am Patient.

When Feeling Confused,
Whisper, I Am Confident.

When Feeling Restless,
Whisper, I Am Calm and I Am Safe.

When Feeling Rejected,
Whisper, I Accept Me and I Am Loved.

When Feeling Stressed, Anxious or Overwhelmed,
Whisper, I Am in Charge of my Peace.

When Feeling Dejected, Hopeless or Depressed,
Whisper, I Am Joy and I Am Resilient.

When Feeling Inferior or Unimportant,
Whisper, I Am Capable and I Am Worthy.

When Feeling Doubtful,
Whisper, I Am Grounded.

When Feeling Humiliation or Shame,
Whisper, I Am Favored and I Am Proud of Myself.

When Feeling Unworthy,
Whisper, I Am Deserving.

When Feeling Inadequate,
Whisper, I Am Able and I Am Good Enough.

When Feeling Angry or Revengeful,
Whisper, I Am in Control.

When Feeling Broken or Bitter,
Whisper, I Am Blessed.

When Feeling Insecure, Incapable or Fearful,
Whisper, I Am Courageous.

When Feeling Helpless,
Whisper, I Am Not Alone.

When Feeling like a Burden or Not Needed,
Whisper, I Am Meaningful and I Am Valuable.

When Feeling like a Mistake, Unwanted or Disposable,
Whisper, I Am a Gift.

Mother Earth

She is fierce.
She cries.

She demands respect.
She is an old soul
with empath eyes.

She is temperamental.
She is rich.

She rests.
She is climactic.

She dots.
She joyfully sings.

She is organically perfect.
She is the impetus
for yearning wings.

She is patient.
She tenderly smiles.

She is timeless.
She tantrums
like an insolent child.

She births life.
She knows no fear.

She is not only
water, earth and fire,
but most importantly, she is air.

She beams with delight,
glowing in breathless sunsets and
shimmering in glorious sunrises.

She embodies the
aura of a gentle loon.

She is Mother
to those tender buds
that magically bloom.

She fights blind battles.
She is a majestic Queen.

She quenches droughts.
She is the rustle and sway
in vibrant autumn trees.

She is a gift.
She is hope.

She is unconditional.
She is an ethereal vision to behold.

A Shell of a Soul

I was just a shell of a soul,
existing in only one mode.
Felt unseen, not heard,
not valued, not loved.
Waiting for the rainbows, falling stars and
heavens to whisper my divine purpose
but sadly no word from above.

I looked for me in all the wrong places.
I looked for family in the unlikeliest of spaces.
Who decided my name?
From where is my tribe?
Why did you want me?
When will it become apparent that
it's in my arms of my destiny where I need to run.

Stillness has helped me find my voice.
Stillness has helped me discover who I am.
I'm finally trusting my steps.
I've quelled my fears to be accepting of God's master plan.

Survive

See you through unconditional eyes,
while dreaming of better tomorrows
during quintessential nights.

Never compromise your value or your worth,
as you walk healed of your wounds and
repaired from your brokenness.

Leave a path of glitter wherever you go,
while empowering encountered souls
to embrace their glow.

Be a warrior during unprecedented vortices
while entrusting your higher self
to direct its transcending metamorphosis.

Never concede, self-pity or exhaust a good cry
as you live with no regrets
and as you spread your wings and fly.

Stand like ancestors gone, while breathing in faith,
knowing that you're never alone.
Embrace "I am" like God's ever-present clouds,
as you fight to survive
while donning that gifted crown.

My Insecurities (Boys)

I will no longer
be embarrassed
about my name,
my prominent nose,
my hairy toes,
my love-struck eyes,
my inability to lie,
my patchy skin,
my journey to be a king,
my sun kissed freckles,
my coke bottle spectacles,
my nervous stutter,
my love for my mother,
my dumbo ears,
my crocodile tears,
my contagious laugh,
my fascination of cats,
my knock knees,
my gapped teeth,
my carrot top,
my dreads or my locs,
my love of science,
my gentle shyness,
my dialect,
my anxiety before a test,
my scrawny arms and my geeky charm.
Why? Because God made me this way.

Power

Power comes from the ability to walk in the Light until the very end.
Power comes from courageously Surrendering perceived control
while allowing one's hurts to mend.

Power comes from refusing to embrace the Insanity in this dreamscape World.
Power comes from walking as scholarly Boys and Girls.

Power comes from opening the hearts of Nonbelievers to their Precious Gifts.
Power comes from empowering Souls whose lives are aimlessly Adrift.

Power comes by modeling Love to Hearts in despair.
Power comes from Walking with Clarity which can only be gained through
Meditation, Introspection and Prayer.

Power comes from the ability to Unite
by embodying Peace.
Power comes from Bridging the Gaps
as you plant yielding yet majestic trees.

Power comes from Relinquishing generationally conditioned Truths.
Power comes from owning the organic Empath in you.

Power comes from knowing one's Reason for being.
Power comes from impacting throughout life's seasons.

Power comes from offering Infinite words of hope.
Power comes from growing, blooming and blossoming through one's growth.

Power comes from allowing Eternal spirits to lead one's every step.
Power comes from purposefully, faithfully and passionately
Living life until one's last Breath.

I Want to Apologize
(From Dads Around the World)

I want to apologize for my absence, insensitivity, uncaring ways
and stubborn pride.
I want to apologize for overwhelming your spirit
with habitual let downs and overt lies.

I want to apologize for the toxic things you've seen and heard
and for your struggles, nightmares and woes.
I want to apologize for walls of arrogant and hurtful words
and for being heartless, hard to love and cold.

I want to apologize for not making you feel like the apple of my eye.
I want to apologize for not being there to teach you and to show you
wrong from right.

I want to apologize for not treasuring and appreciating
my precious gifts.
I want to apologize for not cultivating an ethereal princess
and a refined prince.

I want to apologize for not finishing what I started, not being there to
dry your tears or hold your hand.
I want to apologize for walking away from my responsibilities and
for not showing you the heart, the face and the soul of a decent and
valiant man.

I want to apologize for not being there for every step of your journey
because of my selfish and narcissistic ways.
I want to apologize for not being your mom's king, but you know what,
I would've done her an injustice if I stayed.

I want to apologize for not being there for the father-daughter dances and not showing up for any of your games.
I want to apologize for not being there to motivate and support your visions and dreams but instead filling your spirit with guilt, sadness, anger and shame.

I want to apologize for not being there as a shoulder to cry on, thus robbing your ability to laugh, trust and love.
I want to apologize for making you feel unimportant, invisible, unworthy, disposable and not good enough.

I hope this apology allows you to forgive all the pain I've created now that you know my absence wasn't your fault.

I hope this apology allows you to free yourself from my baggage so you can spread your beautiful wings to not only fly,
but more importantly, to soar.

I Want to Apologize (From Moms Around the World)

I want to apologize for not showing you selfless and unconditional love and for my moody, irritable and erratic ways.
I want to apologize for not being there to empower my son or my daughter and for haphazardly, for neglectfully leaving you in the hands of strays.

I want to apologize to your innocent heart for what it had to endure and to your innocent soul for the trauma it had to face.
I want to apologize to your mind for the influx of confusing games and to your voice that was lost along the way.

I want to apologize for abusing the role of a mother and for not healing my broken and wounded spirit.
I want to apologize for not finishing what I started, for listening to, believing in and walking with those subliminal generational lyrics.

I want to apologize for not being there to see you crawl, walk or run because I chose chaos rather than peace, hope and faith.
I want to apologize for not tending to your cuts, hurts or pain, being there for your Easter speeches, seeing you accept your diplomas or witnessing on Christmas morn the glee in your eyes and on your face.

I want to apologize for not nurturing my bundles of joy or acknowledging your blessed presence.
I want to apologize for not being there to cook your favorite meals and for the void from my absence.

I want to apologize for not being there to help you buckle and tie your shoes or to brush and comb your tangled hair.
I want to apologize for choosing my addictions over motherhood,which stole pieces of your life because that just wasn't fair.

I want to apologize for not walking virtuously and for removing
my crown.
I want to apologize for succumbing to worldly traps and not showing
my face despite living in the same town.

I want to apologize for missing out on your milestones, your successes,
your growth spurts, not seeing you go for your dreams, not reading your
favorite bedtime stories and not tucking you in good night.
I want to apologize for making you sniffle, tear, weep and for leaving
without saying good bye.

I want to apologize for not being a devoted Queen that wears and
clutches her heir-loomed pearls.
I want to apologize for not being there for those cherished mother-
daughter tea parties and for watching you laugh and endlessly twirl.

I want to apologize for not possessing a peaceful aura
and for not seeing or believing in this rare bloom.
I want to apologize for not being that sweet sweet ma that catches you
putting on my red lipstick or finding you sneaking my expensive perfume.

I want to apologize for not being your safety net or guardian angel.
I want to apologize for not believing that I was capable or able.

I hope this apology allows you to forgive all the pain I've created now
that you know my absence wasn't your fault.

I hope this apology allows you to free yourself of your baggage,
so you can spread your beautiful wings to not only fly,
but more importantly, to soar.

Gifts From God

Glorious Sunrises
Captivating Eyes
Crimson Sunsets
The Blessing of Life

Free Spirits
Peaceful Rests
Gifted Heartbeats
Serenity at its Best

Foreshadowing Visions
A Summer Breeze
Intuition
Clarity

Unrequited Love
Second Chances
Loyal White Doves
Touching Father-Daughter Dances

Mesmerizing Rainbow
Hypnotic Nature Sounds
The Blessed Day He Arose
Families of Migrating Clouds

Mercy and Grace
Knowing Thy Purposeful Way
Soul's Objectivity
Soothing White Sands
Generosity
Enchanted Romance

Mother Earth
Luminous Stars and Moons
Joyous Births
That Image Staring Back at You

Live

Live Carefully not Recklessly.
Live Selflessly not Egotistically.
Live Honorably not Disgracefully.
Live Credibly not Credulously.
Live Compassionately not Unsympathetically.
Live Virtuously not Nefariously.
Live Courageously not Cowardly.
Live Kindly not Heartlessly.
Live Faithfully not Dubiously.
Live Humbly not Arrogantly.
Live Honestly not Deceitfully.
Live Fairly not Inequitably.
Live Genuinely not Ingeniously.
Live Practically not Illogically.
Live Optimistically not Hopelessly.
Live Sincerely not Snippily.
Live Respectfully not Disrespectfully.
Live Logically not Impulsively.
Live Authentically not Delusively.
Live Joyfully not Gloomily.
Live Peacefully not Anxiously.
Live Responsibly not Haphazardly.
Live Passionately not Apathetically.
Live Wisely not Foolishly.
Live Graciously not Discourteously.
Live Confidently not Meekly.
Live Thankfully not Ungratefully.
LIVE

The New Me

How I walk today will be different
in how I walk in truth tomorrow.
How I feel today will be different
in how I glow tomorrow.
How I exist today will be different
in how I passionately live tomorrow.
How I follow today will be different
in how I lead tomorrow.
What I held onto today,
I will relinquish tomorrow.
What I dream today
will be my Deja vu tomorrow.
What was my crutch today
will be my platform tomorrow.

Only Invite Those into Your World

Only invite those into your world
who embodies love.
Only invite those into your world
whose Visions soar higher than a mourning dove.

Only invite those into your world
who not only support but more importantly
respect, understand and believe in your life calling, journey and Dreams.
Only invite those into your world
who empower you to be a better you.

Only invite those into your world
who challenges sentences that end in but.
Only invite those into your world
whose Heart has your heart's best interest at heart.

Only invite those into your world
who can and will value a true friendship.
Only invite those into your world
who you connect with on a Mental and Spiritual kinship.

Only invite those into your world
who avows your king or queen-ness.
Only invite those into your world
who supports and respects your gifted genius.
Only invite those into your world
who will impact mankind with their
magical purpose.
Only invite those into your world
whose life's Mission is to
make a difference through humbled service.

My Insecurities
(Girls)

I will no longer
be embarrassed
about my name
my thin lips
my wide hips
my crooked nose
my pigeon toes
my lazy eyes
my thick thighs
my patchy skin
my fear of mannequins
my speckled freckles
my coke bottle spectacles
my snorty laugh
my long legs like a giraffe
my dumbo ears
my sappy tears
my love of pink hats
my kinky curly naps
my dialect
my graceful neck
my knock knees
my gapped teeth
my red hair
my locks and my dreads
my book smarts
my tender heart
my quiet kindness
my hidden shyness
my journey and my storms or
my desire to transform.

Why?

Because God made me this way.

You've Found the One

If your love interest
embodies the depth like mother earth,
the gentle mood like air,
the passion like fire and
the calm like water
then you've found the one.

Goodness

Goodness is

humanity,

compassion,

generosity,

empathy,

decency,

integrity,

kindness

and

courage.

Seeds of Difference

Be a bloom from peace.
Be a bloom of kindness.
Be a bloom from humanity.
Be a bloom from color blindness.

Be an honorable King.
Be a regal Queen.
Be a bloom of compassion.
Be a bloom of empathy.

Be self-actualized through reflection.
Be an embodiment of introspection.

Be a bloom of pureness.
Be a bloom from Mother Earth.
Be a bloom from rainbows.
Be a bloom from the spoken word.

Be a meaningful conception.
Live only with intention.

Be a bloom from self-love.
Be a bloom that's risen above.
Be a bloom from the flames.
Be a bloom from the rain.

Be a bloom of hope.
Be a bloom from life's inequities.
Be a seed of difference.
Be a bloom of resiliency.

Ice Cream Cake

Don't let something like ELA stress you out.
Don't let day to day chores get under your skin.
Don't let something like Algebra drive you crazy.
Don't let your little sister or brother get on your nerves.
Don't let something like Science frustrate your brain.
Don't let homework overwhelm your peace.

I figured if I want my favorite desert of Ice cream cake that I have to
rearrange my thoughts and my brain from thinking -

"I can't to I can"
"I'm not to I am"
"I won't to I will"
"Its too hard to I'll try"

Why?

Because,
I know in life,
that people, place and things
can and will annoy, irritate and frustrate me.

I will look beyond me
and do what's right and kind.
If it's a windy day,
I'll ask my little brother or sister
If they want to go fly a kite or play.

I will wake up each morning
with a smile on my face,
joy in my heart and a bounce in my step.

Why?

Because, at the end of each day,
I want to know that I did my very best which
earned me my favorite dessert of ice cream cake.

I Am

I Am Not You.
I Am Me.

I Am No Longer Blind.
Instead, I Walk in Epiphanies.

I Am Not the Reason for your Insanity.
I Am your Reality.

I Am Not your Fate.
Instead, I'm your Destiny.

I Am Not the Ashes after Volcanic Eruptions.
Instead, I Walk Renewed.

I Am Me. I Am Not You.

I Am Not your Past. I Am your Present.
I Am Not a Danger. Instead, I'm Heaven-sent.

I Am Not a Victim. I Am a Survivor.

I Am Not Damaged or Broken.
Instead, I Walk in Purpose,
Love and Faith.

I Am Not your Rescuer or Enabler.
Instead, I'm your Impetus in Wait.

I am Not Invisible.
Instead, I'm a Luminous Star.

I am Not the Remnants after a Storm.
Instead, I'm a Blessing from Above.

I am Not a Burden,
a Mistake or your Pain.
Instead, I'm a Precious Gift like
Quenching Jasmine Rain.

I am Not a Slave. I Am Free.
I Am Not You. I Am Me.

Saving Me

Mom, how could you not defend me?
The one in which your lips boast,
brag and stand on when daggers
aren't being thrown.

Mom, how could you not defend me,
knowing fam, scarred my innocence,
my heart and
my chance at fertility.

Mom, how could you not defend me,
knowing good and well,
fam left a trail of brokenness
during his monstrous rampage.

Mom, wake up, because you're slowly losing my respect,
my honor, my love and my time.

I know what the Bible says about the eyes of an obedient child but this
child of the Almighty will no longer be controlled by whispers from the
grave.

I will now embrace a world of possibilities and new beginnings.

Mom, you've never once dried my tears or supplied my basic needs, but
instead only manipulated my secrets, twisted the truth and justified the
lies.

I am halfway through my life and still donning the scars from my
wounded ness. I've decided I will work as hard as I've ever had to gain
closure to my past.

I now know I am a long overdue project. I proclaim today is the day
to begin investing in me so that I can live in peace. I am your daughter,
and until death, I will provide but I need you to see me.

I can no longer remain quiet to my pain.
I will not walk into another year
under hovering clouds of fear, guilt,
embarrassment and shame.

As I own my clarity, I will not let anyone or anything take me off my
journey to healing and loving my blessings, my life and the sweet,
sweet gifts God was gracious to entrust in me.

The Gift

Never allow a gift to slip through your grasp.
Never stop making her giggle, smile or laugh.

Notice stars that float from her bright trusting eyes.
Notice the sparkling of excited, yet coy butterflies.

Dot and baby your sweet sweet honey love.
Honor the devotion of conjoined swans.
Model the tenderness of ethereal kissing doves.

Reminisce of the first day she made your heart flutter.
Reminisce of when you knew she was like no other.

Create beautiful moments in between each Anniversary.
Bloom magical years and unforgettable memories.

Breathe in peace as you sight see in city carriages.
Walk blessed from when she said yes to your proposal of marriage.

Walk gratefully, tickled and filled with
pure joy knowing you'll peer into eyes that only dream of you,
when you enter those sanctuary doors.

Be thankful for your little piece of heaven.
Be thankful for every second spent with your happily ever after.

I Want to Apologize (To My Soul)

I Want to Apologize, To My Soul, For Not…

Loving It
Growing It
Honoring It
Balancing It
Nurturing It

Breathing Life Into It
Listening To It
Feeding It
Praying For It
Valuing It

Empowering It
Being Kind To It
Cultivating It
Trusting It
Caring For It

Blooming It
Respecting It
Grounding It
Treasuring It &
Saving It.

I Apologize.

Dont Wait for a COVID 19

Don't wait for a COVID 19
...to capture glorious crimson skies or to
marvel at whimsical yellow butterflies.

Don't wait for a COVID 19
...to get lost in surprising moons or to tend to infinite hues of blue.

Don't wait for a COVID 19
...to realize that every beat of one's heart has been gifted by a Son so
sweet, so loving and so kind or to write resolutions and intentions for
your precious time.

Don't wait for a COVID 19
...to authentically embrace every minute of every day or to sit in
quietness and allow for healing during those reflective rains.

Don't wait for a COVID 19
...to porch swing and reminisce every chance you get or to realize that
this thing called Life is a literal and a figurative test.

Celebrate

*Start your New Years off proper by making a good luck pot of Hop N Johns, Collard Greens and Sweet Potato Soufflé with plump Candied Raisins.

*Capture, honor and treasure each gifted and blessed occasion.

*Celebrate MLK Day by listening to his inspiring, "I Have a Dream" speech.

*Make Valentine goodie bags for your kids which will surely make them gleam.

*See who can organize and clean their bedroom the fastest, as a family night game.

*Wear your favorite shade of green and a four-leaf clover on that festive St. Patrick's Day.

*Answer your kid's questions about the life, resurrection and miracles of Christ.

*Have an Easter egg hunt, in the backyard, before dawn meets nigh.

*Make mom a special Mother's Day brunch and serve it to her in bed.

*Give dad a homemade Father's Day card no matter where he lays his head.

*Read the Declaration of Independence on the 4th of July and print one for everyone in the house.

*Have your own fall carnival filled with games and yummy delights while the little ones joyfully run about.

*Call or video chat with family and friends after a belly full of your favorite Thanksgiving fixins.

*Go for a morning and evening stroll to ensure healthy, reflective and balanced living.

*Adorn your home with red, green and silver tinsel so that Santa won't get lost.

*Walk in gratitude, humility and love because Jesus died for mankind sins on that Holy cross.

At My Wits End

Love them
through their trials,
love them
compassionately but with intentional eyes,
love them
through their growing pains,
love them
as you break free of toxic generational chains,
love them
in the face of uncertainty,
love them
to their destiny,
love them
when all else fails,
love them
when they fight you tooth and nail,
love them
because you have enough love for two,
love them
because they are every bit a part of you,
love them
from the depth of your soul,
love them
through those day's of hot and cold,
love them
as God loves us,
love them
as you walk in faith, hope, patience and trust.

Words to Help Kids Fly

Rise and Shine
Maintain a Positive Mind
Always Have a Great Day
In School You Must Stay
Do a Good Job
Know It's Okay to Sob
Be a Good Friend
See Life through Until the End
Tell the Truth
Believe in You
Know You are a Gift
Always Motivate, Inspire and Uplift
Never Give Up
Know You are Loved
Try your very Best
Ace each Test
Glow like a Firefly
Don't Get Stuck with Why
Grow like a Fragrant Dandelion
Pump Iron
Rise like the Sun
Know that Learning can be Fun
Think like a Scholar
Make an Honest Dollar
Bloom
Know it's Cool to Just be You
Wear your Crown
Make yourself Proud
Soar
Face all of life's Doors
Work as a Team
Be a Teacher's Dream.

Just like a Flower

Just like a flower needs
sunshine and rain,
a child needs unconditional love and
attention to bloom and to change.

Just like a flower needs
sweet songs and kind words,
a child needs to be seen, validated,
attaboys and to be heard.

Just like a flower needs tender,
loving care, a child needs to be raised
in a home that is firm yet fair.

Just like a flower needs butterflies and bees,
a child needs to be taught and
role modeled the principles of
patience, respect and honesty.

Just like a flower needs
sunrises and sunsets,
a child needs Mother Nature's
Vitamin D and the right amount of rest.

Just like a flower needs
a name to be known,
a child needs a special,
warm, sweet and peaceful
place to call their home.

The Game

Young folks,
put your energy into the
academic and skill game

and not

The Drug Game
The Gang Game
The Fast Life Game
The Peer Pressure Game
The Fame Game
The Challenge Game
The Power Game
The Clout Game
The Pimpin' Game
The Street Game and
The Drop Out Game.

Know that you are ultimately in control of your life.

A Friend

A friend is someone who will be there
during one's highs and one's lows
&
during life's yeses and nos.

A friend is someone who will be there
during one's successes and one's failures
&
during one's regressive and one's stagnant behaviors.

A friend is someone who will be there
during one's good days and bad
&
during life's moments of happy and sad.

A friend is someone who will be there
during one's losses and one's gains
&
during life's joys and pain.

A friend is someone who will be there
during one's trials and one's tribulations
&
during life's most difficult situations.

A friend is someone who will be there
during one's lapses of judgement
&
during one's fear based reluctance.

A fiend is someone who will be
there during one's celebratory moments
&
during one's need for endorsements.

A friend is someone who will be there
during one's sicknesses and one's times of need
& during one's period of mourning, loss and grief.

Cherish your friends.

Even If

Even if you weren't born
with a silver spoon in your mouth, so what.

Don't let a silver spoon
define your heart or your dreams.

A Little Piece of Heaven

Sitting in quietness
at the week's end,
away from the world's angry chatter,
being moved by Caruso's Dalla,
soothed by Bach's Air on a G String,
captivated by Chopin's Nocturne in C Sharp,
transcended by Mozart's Concerto for Clarinet,
inspired by Puccini's Nessun Dorma and
enveloped by Rachmaninoff's
Second Piano Concerto.

Heaven.

COVID-19

Frontline heroes.
Quarantines.
Marshaled states.
An introvert's dream.

Hovering blankets.
Broken dams.
Social distancing.
The measure of a man.

Eerie ghost towns.
Empty dinner chairs.
Historic casualties.
A Germaphobes worst nightmare.

Distracting skies.
No where to run.
Unprecedented times.
Frantic efforts to safeguard the
ones we love.

Empathy and transparency
is a want and a need.
Stimulus overload.
A new normal for swirling souls
blindsided by 2020.

Makeshift hospitals.
Anticipated vaccine.
Remote learning.
Crushed hopes...shelved dreams.

Final breaths...
of angels who got their wings.
Lessons and tests...
while praying to the lord of lords
and
to the king of kings.

A time to get one's house in
order...
for signs are everywhere.
A time to shine with decency,
kindness and
humanity as they must prevail over
fear.

Now rest...for this too shall pass.

2020

Empaths in a vacillating tailspin,
resting on faith and not on the words
of men who just want to be king.

The world's shifting energies
was too much to contain,
splitting at the seams,
a dizzying vortex
but gifts manage to
comfort those
in search of peace-
in search of rainbows.

Brace yourself,
as this new normal
isn't going away.

Catch each tear.
Push through all the fears and know
that 2020 was written before your 1st breath.

Maybe

Maybe Covid 19 happened for husbands and wives to repair broken promises and dishonored vows.
Maybe Covid 19 happened for the world to set their eyes upon restorative and watchful clouds.

Maybe Covid 19 happened so that families could rebuild, create timeless memories and reconnect.
Maybe Covid 19 happened so one could pause and ask yourself, "Why am I allowing this abuse, more abuse, more abuse and neglect?"

Maybe Covid 19 happened to shake up this all
con-sumptuous, fast paced and frazzled world.
Maybe Covid 19 happened for you to take the time to
gaze in the mirror at that special, rare and precious pearl.

Maybe Covid 19 happened to redirect misguided and idled potentials.
Maybe Covid 19 happened to remind us that the only things we are truly in control of is our memories created from soul encounters, our legacy and our collective reactions.

Don't Stop

Don't stop writing.
Don't stop growing.
Don't stop fighting.
Don't stop glowing.
Don't stop breathing.
Don't stop singing.
Don't stop healing.
Don't stop living.
Don't stop sharing.
Don't stop dancing.
Don't stop caring.
Don't stop laughing.
Don't stop creating.
Don't stop asserting.
Don't stop relating.
Don't stop exerting.
Don't stop dreaming.
Don't stop praying.
Don't stop believing.
Don't stop repaying.
Don't stop enacting.
Don't stop mothering.
Don't stop impacting.
Don't stop loving.

Don't Stop

Desire

As you journey through this thing
called life,
create inspiring words of wisdom,
idioms, meditations and proverbs
that move you to live
a life of desire and intention.

Desire to feed, nurture and soothe
one's soul with mindful and
restorative
calming breaths.

Desire to cleanse, free and save
self
by speaking ugly buried truths.

Desire to free one's soul
from blinding lies
and haunting whispers of
invaluableness.

Desire to put in the work
to strengthen one's
fragile and battled mental,
physical and spiritual core.

Desire to reclaim
one's stolen innocence,
one's stolen memory,
one's stolen childhood,
and one's stolen worth.

Desire to mend
bandaged wounds and harbored
cracks.

Desire to give oneself permission
to unblock imbalances
from the soles of one's feet
to the crown of one's head.

Desire to feel.
Desire to live.
Desire to be your absolute best.

Desire.

Self-Love

Despite of and in spite of those
temporal, occipital, parietal
and frontal exposures,
know that you are now free
to be all that you want to be and
all that others said you won't.

No one can heal you but you.
Peer into the deepest facets
of your fear in order to blossom
into an authentically beautiful
butterfly.

Break up with sabotaging
self-deprecation, self-doubt, self-
loathing,
self-hatred and low self-worth.

Breathe in hope when torn,
lost, worn or reflecting upon
embedded whispers
that tried to control your destiny,
destroy your faith and silence your
truth.

Look in the mirror, everyday and
smile.
Give yourself permission to be the
director over not only the middle,
but more importantly,
the ending to your life story.

Men, walk as honorable, humble
and noble Kings. Women, soar as
worthy, virtuous and
regal Queens.
Be that passionate,
peaceful and pure bloom.
Grow with your seeds.
Glow in your tribe and
show your creator
that each blessed breath,
that each gifted heartbeat and
that each purported step
will not be in vain.

When Stressed

When stressed,

Paint
Walk
Laugh
Meditate
Journal
Draw and Color
Call a Friend
Dance
Pray
Cloud Watch
Read an Inspiring Book
Breathe
Rest
and
Sing
because you and only you are in charge of
your peace, the nurturance of your mind/body and-
soul, your sanity and your day to day joy.

I Just Love You

I love your infectious spirit.
I love your intentional eyes.
I love your unique swag.
I love the warmth of your endearing smile.

I love the depth of your soul.
I love the tenderness of your heart.
I love your humbling grace.
I love your beautiful works of art.

I love the way you love me.
I love that you took that chance.
I love our favorite love songs.
I love our aura when we slow dance.

I love your chivalry and your honor.
I love your passionate drive.
I love your helping hands.
I love how you give me space to fly.

I love the passion in your words.
I love your zestful joy.
I love your ingenious mind.
I love when you, not only give life, but more importantly us, your all.

I love the victory of your journey.
I love that you stand in your truth.
I love your easy breeziness.
I just love you.

Desire To Be

Desire to be
a dreamer
an achiever
a believer
a leader.
Desire to be
a catalyst
an activist
an impetus
an optimist.

Desire to be
a peacemaker
a trailblazer
a change maker
an encourager.

Desire to be
a motivator
a conqueror
a problem solver
a messenger
Desire to be
a vessel
a pioneer
an advocate
a hero.

Desire to be.

Grounding Mantras

(I Am Safe)
(I Am A Gift)
(I Am Worthy)
(I Am Imperfect)
(I Am Calm)
(I Am Forgiven)
(I Am A Survivor)
(I Am Good Enough)
(I Am a Voice)
(I Am Here)
(I Am Now)
(I Am Balanced)
(I Am at Peace)
(I Am Joy)
(I Am Love)
(I Am Free)
(I Am Safe)
(I Am A Gift)
(I Am Worthy)
(I Am Imperfect)
(I Am Calm)
(I Am Forgiven)
(I Am A Survivor)
(I Am Good Enough)
(I Am a Voice)
(I Am Here)
(I Am Now)
(I Am Balanced)
(I Am at Peace)
(I Am Joy)
(I Am Love)
(I Am Free)

I Write

I write because
I have a baby to birth.
I write because
I know my sacred worth.

I write because
I have a gift to share.
I write because
I am no longer stifled by fear.

I write because
it is life that I choose.
I write because
I can't contain a passion
that must blossom and bloom.

I write
what I feel and what I see.
I write because
I am no longer afraid to exist
authentically.

I write because
my knowledge is like gold.
I write because
my words are enlightening,
healing and empowering mantras
for the soul.

I write because
I've been saved from the flames.
I write because
I'm awestricken by the surreal ness
of
each and every day.

I write
to share truths of the living.
I write because
it's a blessing that keeps on giving.

I write because
I'm drawn by my calling.
I write to be an impetus, a
motivator and
a catalyst for the mourning.

I write because
God sacrificed, so 'I Can.'
I write because
God showed me, that 'I Am.'

The Knowledge

As a messenger of knowledge,
I accept the call

to Reconnect
to Empower
to Unite and
to Inspire Timid Buds to Flower

to Repair
to Heal
to Free
to Reveal

to Rebuild
to Save
to Restore
to Awake

to Empathize
to Balance
to Love
to Challenge

Respect

Respect your birth
Respect your value and your worth
Respect your intuition
Respect your mission's vision
Respect your blessings
Respect life's lessons
Respect your ride or die family
Respect the situations gravity
Respect your talents and your gifts
Respect the reason you may exist
Respect the process
Respect your progress
Respect your temple
Respect your mental
Respect your neighbors
Respect your Lord & Savior
Respect your hopes and dreams
Respect your destiny.

Promises to Me

As I innately do for others,
I will do for me.

I will unapologetically love and nurture
every soul encounter to spread hope in
every season.

I will listen with compassion and empathy.
I will dream, breathe and live mindfully.

I will embrace a life of
I Will, I Can and I Am until eternity.
I will only befriend others
who possesses like minded reciprocity,
genuine authenticity
and emotional availability.

I will sleep soundly.
I will move among the birthed fearlessly.

I will speak my truth and share my
story because there is true beauty in vulnerability.

I will maintain a mental, physical and spiritual lifestyle of balance
as I honor my purpose with authenticity.

Who I Am

I Am Joy.
I Am Peace.
I Am Love.
I Am Free.

I Am a Gift.
I Am Living Unapologetically.
I Am a Rare Bloom.
I Am Standing Enlightened in Epiphanies.

I Am Balance.
I Am Living the Dream.
I Am Aglow.
I Am Growing Wisely.

I Am a Treasure.
I Am Faithful.
I Am Healed.
I Am Able.

I Am Continuously Transcending.
I Am Excited About Life.
I Am Designed for Greatness.
I Am Restored by the Night.

I Am Here to Make a Difference.
I Am Walking in My Worth.
I Am Timeless.
I Am a Vessel of Mother Earth.

Then We Can Cheer

When racism and hate is extinct,
When discrimination and prejudice is extinct,
When sexism and ageism is extinct,
When gun and gang violence is extinct,
When domestic violence and abuse is extinct,
When terrorism and barbarism is extinct,
When racial profiling and inequality is extinct,
When dictatorship and totalitarianism is extinct,
When police brutality and racial disparity is extinct,
When false imprisonment and injustice is extinct,
When segregation and multicultural insensitivity is extinct,
When racial inequality and slavery is extinct,
When wrath, envy and jealousy is extinct,
When homelessness and hunger is extinct,
When social classes and inflation are extinct,
When cancer, juvenile diabetes and sickle cell anemia is extinct,
When war and genocide is extinct,
When man's inhumanity to man is extinct ...

Then We Can Cheer!

Freedom is Empowering

Freedom is empowering when you preserve your spirit, your aura & your energy.

Freedom is empowering when you embrace faith, joy & tranquility.

Freedom is empowering when you value balance, friendships & life's blessings.

Freedom is empowering when you listen to the Universe, honor your village and learn
from life's lessons.

Freedom is empowering when you embody gratitude, empathy & humility.

Freedom is empowering when you own your strengths, bloom your creativity and are cognizant that there is beauty in vulnerability.

Freedom is empowering when you run into the arms of your dreams, your purpose &
your destiny.

Freedom is empowering when you take time out to relax, meditate & breathe.

Freedom is empowering when you reclaim your power, your voice and your peace.
Freedom is empowering when you aren't afraid of evolving, blossoming & new beginnings.

Freedom is empowering when you know that there is more to life than winning.

Freedom is empowering when you know you can dream, soar & fly.

Freedom is empowering when you nurture your body, soul & mind.

Freedom is empowering when you
glow, grow & bloom.

Freedom is empowering when you give yourself permission to replenish,
restore & renew.

Freedom is empowering when you not only care for but more
importantly care about your
fellow man.

Freedom is empowering when you believe
I Will, I Am & I Can.

Glow with Purpose

Dream with Purpose.
Wake with Purpose.
Walk with Purpose.
Grow with Purpose.
Talk with Purpose.
Think with Purpose.
Live with Purpose.
Move with Purpose.
Partner with Purpose.
Glow with Purpose.

I Am No One's Illusion

I Am Gratefully Blessed.
I Am Not My Scars.
I Am a Gift.
I Am One of God's Brightest Stars.

I Am Fearless.
I Am Free.
I Am Love.
I Am Authentically Me.

I Am a Worthy Queen.
I Am A Free-Spirited Soul.
I Am Joy.
I Am a Rare Red Rose.

I Am an Honorable King.
I Am an Agent of Peace.
I Am a Fearless yet Humble Ruler.
I Am a Man of Dignity.

I Am an Angelic Butterfly.
I Am an Empowered Being.
I Am a Survivor.
I Am a Beautiful Dream.

I Am Enough.
I Am Human.
I Am Living My Best Life.
I Am No One's Illusion.

I Love Me More

I love you but I love me more.
I now know that I was in love
with the idea of love and
that is just not enough.

I will love someone who is healed
and values self-love.

I will love someone who knows
and honors the concept of true love.

I will only invite a love interest into my life whose capabilities meet my
needs.

I will only invite a love interest into my life who knows how to love,
respect, nurture
and feed my soul.

I will save me, my destiny, my dreams, my peace, my sanity and my
dignity.

I will save my seeds so they won't stand or walk in fallible footsteps.

I will deprogram my heartbeats
from thinking it's okay and
normal to be dishonorable, inauthentic, emotionally unavailable, insecure,
unaccountable and a broken being.

I now know, with the help of my higher power, my saving grace and my
blessing in disguise that I am deserving, I am worthy, I am a gift,
I am a king, I am a queen,
I am a blossom of Mother Earth,

I am heaven-sent,
I am a survivor, I am valuable,
I am capable and I am complete.

To save me, I will reject the fear of rejection,
I will abandon the fear of abandonment,
I will drown out echoing whispers from broken souls, I will curse the
idea that I don't matter,
I will let go of generational toxicity,
I will walk in my purpose,
I will unapologetically love and nurture me,
I will divorce lies of being inadequate and
I will wave goodbye to the unrecognizable me.

I am thankful I awoke with clarity and a new sense of direction over my
life.

In spite of all my trials,
I will turn my pain into a beautiful and timeless passion that impacts
those
who are walking in my shoes.

I Want to Apologize,
(From Fragile Minds)

I want to apologize for inviting
loathsome depression thus
deterring the embodiment
of forgiveness and tender
compassion.

I want to apologize for
overwhelming you with fearful
and painful memories that
cautioned openness to true and
meaningful friendships.

I want to apologize for the
weighing trials you've had to
endure thus refraining permission
to embrace a spirit that's trusting
and pure.

I want to apologize for inundating
your mind with negative and
criticizing self-talk which didn't
allow for you to affirm you along
your journey's walk.

I want to apologize for the
intrusive guilt, blame and shame
and for not allowing you
to honor the meaning of your
name.

I want to apologize for existing
under a cloud of wrath, revenge
and rage
and for not allowing in the light
on the brightest of days.

I want to apologize for making
you feel undeserving,
invaluable, less than and unworthy
and for not showing you the
reflection,
of a gift, through insightful clarity.

I want to apologize for inflicting
decades of
self-hate, self-pity and self-
deprecation
and for not empowering you
to only look inward for validation.

I want to apologize for living in
the past thus giving your joy away
and for not blooming, growing
and glowing the new you that is
now here to stay.

The Delicate Parts of You

Only entrust
your crown-your joy-your peace,
your happiness & your seeds,
your gifts-your compassion,
your love that's everlasting,
your worth-your empathy,
your hurts & your energy,
your value-your dreams,
the inner essence of your being,
your body-your time,
your heart & your mind,
your soul-your doting attention,
your hopes & your investments,
your visions-your faith and
your virtue & your pain
with a partner
whose capable
of nurturing
the vulnerable,
the special and
the delicate parts of you.

Be

The mother you aren't,
I will be that to my seeds.

The damaged baggage you carry,
I will not claim it as part of my
legacy.

The lies imposed on my tribe,
I will repurpose it with my hands.

The grandmother you aren't,
I will be that blessing to my
grands.

The balance you struggled to gain,
I will embrace it for the sake of
my soul.

The strength you don't possess,
I will nurture it as I blossom,
bloom and grow.

The serenity you never breathed,
I will cherish it for my peace.

The clarity that you muddled,
I will embody it for my dreams.

The king that lay dormant,
I will cultivate him along life's way.

The person you tried to break,
will be saved by God's mercy and
grace.

The wounds you won't heal,
I will not allow it to destroy,
silence or define me.

The queen you refuse to see,
I will be.

Unnecessary Things

Domestic Violence ain't necessary.
Crime ain't necessary.
Jealousy ain't necessary.
Gun Violence ain't necessary.
Injustice ain't necessary.
Denigration of our land ain't necessary.
Racism ain't necessary.
Rivalry ain't necessary.
War ain't necessary.
Divisiveness ain't necessary.
Envy ain't necessary.

So Why?

Poetry

Poetry should empower, blossom and flower— heal and be authentically real. Poetry is the gust in the breeze and the rustle in autumn trees. Poetry is literal and figurative; is a gift and freeing. Poetry rises from the dust and rests in mango suns. Poetry rebirths like fire, water, air and earth. Poetry is pure like a dove, it unites, its love. Poetry is graceful, it's classical, it's modern, it's magical. Poetry is elegant, it's contemporary, it's reminiscent, it's revolutionary. Poetry is a song that speaks of society's beauty and of society's wrongs. Poetry is gentle, it soothes, it consoles, it's you. Poetry whispers truths from and to one's soul. Poetry will never tire or ever grow old.

Summary

I hope the poems in Bloom give hope during these unprecedented and precarious days, offers clarity during times of stagnation, redirect misguided steps, inspire budding poets waiting to share their gifts with the world and feed the souls of those needing a mental and spiritual escape.

Continue blooming, growing and bloosoming.

Author

Terri McCrea is a native of Charleston, South Carolina. She has provided counseling for the past 31 years (23 years of that in private practice). She graduated from St. Andrews Parish High School and the College of Charleston before receiving her Master's Degree in Clinical Counseling from The Citadel. She is an Adjunct Professor, a Licensed Addiction Counselor, a Licensed Professional Counselor, a Licensed Professional Counselor Supervisor and served as a Continuing Education provider for the South Carolina Board for Licensed Professional Counselors, Social Workers, Marital and Family Therapists, Psychologists and Psycho-educational Specialists. She conducts local and national workshops on her 21 books as well as a Life Skills Summer Camp (ages five to eighteen), parenting classes, domestic violence classes and anger management classes. She is the Outreach Coordinator of the Old Bethel United Methodist Church's Community Outreach Program. This platform provides preventative, educational, rehabilitative, counseling, and evangelistic services to the Low Country's at-risk youths, families (including the elderly, poor, imprisoned, homeless, disabled and indigent).

Terri writes mental health articles for local magazines and newspapers. She guest appears for mental health segments on local radio and television networks. She can be described as a coach, counselor, visionary, poet, free spirit and believer that everyone and everything has a purpose. She is a member of the Poetry Society of South Carolina (PSSC), the International African American Museum, Old Bethel United Methodist Choir, Gamma Xi Omega Chapter of Alpha Kappa Alpha Sorority, Inc. and is a proud aunt and grand aunt.

Terri is available for book signings, charity events, public/motivational speaking engagements, workshop facilitation, interviews, expert appearances (radio, web, television and podcast) and poetry readings. She has self-published seven self-help guidebooks, two inspirational guides for couples in love, four empowering guides for tots/tweens/teens, a book of wedding vows (English/Spanish translation), a parent-teacher guide, a mantra, proverbs and intentions book, a how-to-date book and two collections of poetry.

Terri L. McCrea's Books

- The Power of Forgiveness: A Step by Step Guide on How to Let Go, Move On and Begin Living

- A Teacher's Dream: A Goal Setting Guide for Tots and Tweens

- Problem Solving One on One: Proactive Tactics for Millennium Youths

- The Joy of Living: Manifesting a Passionate, Purposeful and Positive You

- When You Fly: The Quintessential Guide for Becoming a Present, Centered and Proper Parent

- When You Fly: The Quintessential Guide for Becoming a Mentally, Physically, Spiritually and Authentically Aligned Person

- When You Fly: The Quintessential Guidebook on How to Become an Emotionally Available, Authentic and Accountable Partner

- When You Fly: The Quintessential Guide for Becoming a Well-Balanced, Well-Aware and Well-Rounded Pupil

- I Will Be…(Inspirational Quotes from Men of Honor, In Love and Walking in their Purpose)

- I Will Be…(Inspirational Quotes from Women of Faith, in Love and Standing in their Worth)

- It's Ok for Boys to…

- It's Ok for Girls to…

- Intentions

- The Book of Mantras: 100 Affirmations to Reframe your Thoughts and Retrain your Brain

- Walk Like a King: 100 Virtues of a True Gentleman

- Elite Girls Wear Pearls: 100 Virtues of Strong, Empowered and Balanced Women

- Powerful Pearls of Wisdom, Meditations, Idioms and Poignant Proverbs to Live By

- Soul Encounters: The Collective Poetry of Terri L. McCrea (2007-2020)

- Bloom: Poems that Speak to One's Soul

- Walking in Love: Wedding Vows for that Special Day

- 2003. 2004, 2nd Edition 2008, What Price Are You Willing to Pay for Love? (Author house: ISBN: 1-418-6299-3 (e-book)

Terri L. McCrea, M.Ed., LAC, LPC, LPC/S
1643B Savannah Hwy, Suite 113,
Charleston, SC 29407
(main) 843.437.7572
(facsimile) 843.763.7202
poeticexpressions@att.net

*Visit: www.btol.com
www.Amazon.com
www.Alibris.com
www.Abebooks.com

Bloom

www.ingramcontent.com/pod-product-compliance
Lightning Source LLC
Chambersburg PA
CBHW072207090426
42740CB00012B/2429